THE SPACE RACE

ASTRONAUTS AND COSMONAUTS

BY
JOHN HAMILTON

Abdo & Daughters
An imprint of Abdo Publishing | abdobooks.com

abdobooks.com

Published by Abdo Publishing, a division of ABDO, PO Box 398166, Minneapolis, Minnesota 55439. Copyright © 2019 by Abdo Consulting Group, Inc. International copyrights reserved in all countries. No part of this book may be reproduced in any form without written permission from the publisher. Abdo & Daughters™ is a trademark and logo of Abdo Publishing.

Printed in the United States of America, North Mankato, Minnesota.
122018
012019

 THIS BOOK CONTAINS RECYCLED MATERIALS

Editor: Sue Hamilton
Copy Editor: Bridget O'Brien
Graphic Design: John Hamilton
Cover Design: Candice Keimig and Pakou Moua
Cover Photo: NASA
Interior Images: Alamy, p. 25. All others NASA.

Library of Congress Control Number: 2018949998
Publisher's Cataloging-in-Publication Data
Names: Hamilton, John, author.
Title: Astronauts and cosmonauts / by John Hamilton.
Description: Minneapolis, Minnesota : Abdo Publishing, 2019 | Series: The space race | Includes online resources and index.
Identifiers: ISBN 9781532118296 (lib. bdg.) | ISBN 9781532171543 (ebook)
Subjects: LCSH: Astronauts--Juvenile literature. | Cosmonauts--Juvenile literature. | Space race--Juvenile literature.
Classification: DDC 629.45--dc23

CONTENTS

NEIL ARMSTRONG

N eil Armstrong (1930–2012) commanded the Apollo 11 NASA Moon mission. Traveling with Armstrong were fellow astronauts Edwin "Buzz" Aldrin and Michael Collins. On July 20, 1969, Armstrong descended to the Moon along with Aldrin in the *Eagle* lunar module. They were aiming for a smooth region called the Sea of Tranquility.

As the *Eagle* dropped closer to the Moon, Armstrong became alarmed. The landing site was strewn with boulders big enough to destroy their spacecraft. Armstrong relied on all his past skills as an astronaut, naval aviator, and test pilot. Always cool under pressure, he took over manual control of the *Eagle* and expertly flew it to a safer area. With their fuel levels critically low, the spaceship finally touched down gently on the Moon's surface. "Houston," Armstrong radioed back to Earth, "Tranquility Base here. The *Eagle* has landed."

FIRST ON THE MOON

Astronaut Neil Armstrong became the first human to set foot on the Moon on July 20, 1969.

X-15

As a test pilot in the early 1960s, Neil Armstrong flew the X-15 rocket plane at NASA's Flight Research Center at Edwards Air Force Base, California (renamed the Neil A. Armstrong Flight Research Center today).

Neil A. Armstrong was born on his grandparents' farm on August 5, 1930, near the small town of Wapakoneta, Ohio. His father took him on an airplane ride when he was six years old. That was when he knew he wanted to be a pilot. Armstrong earned his pilot license by age 16, even before he had a driver's license. He also became an Eagle Scout in the Boy Scouts of America.

Armstrong studied aeronautical engineering for two years at Indiana's Perdue University before becoming a Navy pilot in 1949. At age 20, he was the youngest pilot in his squadron. He flew 78 combat missions during the Korean War.

After his military career, Armstrong finished his college degree and then became a civilian test pilot. He worked for a government group called the National Advisory Committee for Aeronautics (NACA). In 1958, it became part of the National Aeronautics and Space Administration (NASA). Armstrong flew more than 200 different aircraft, including the X-15 rocket plane. It was a record-setting aircraft that flew very high at more than 4,500 miles per hour (7,242 kph).

During his years as a test pilot, Armstrong developed a reputation for quick thinking under stress. He calmly used his scientific knowledge and strong instincts to get himself out of dangerous situations. In 1962, NASA chose him as part of their second group of astronauts. He commanded the Gemini 8 mission in 1966, flying into space with astronaut David Scott. They were the first astronauts to dock two vehicles together in orbit.

Armstrong's second trip into space came in 1969, when he commanded the Apollo 11 mission. After skillfully piloting the lunar module *Eagle* to the surface, he became the first person to set foot on the Moon. He radioed back to Earth, "That's one small step for a man, one giant leap for mankind."

Armstrong retired from NASA shortly after the Apollo 11 mission. He became a college professor and a businessman. He hated bragging about his achievements in space, preferring instead to thank the thousands of men and women at NASA who helped make his moonwalk possible. Neil Armstrong died on August 25, 2012, from complications he suffered after heart surgery. He was 82.

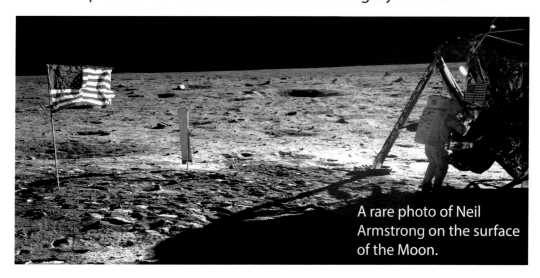

A rare photo of Neil Armstrong on the surface of the Moon.

YURI GAGARIN

Vostok 1 liftoff

On April 12, 1961, from the Baikonur Cosmodrome in Kazakhstan, a powerful rocket roared to life, launching 27-year-old cosmonaut Yuri Gagarin (1934–1968) into the history books. The moment he lifted off, Gagarin excitedly said, "Poyekhali!" ("Let's go!") That day, he became the first human to travel in space. As the sole crew member aboard the Soviet Union's Vostok 1 spacecraft, Gagarin was also the first person to orbit the Earth.

Yuri Gagarin was born in a small farming village in western Russia. In the 1950s, he learned to fly jets in the Soviet Air Forces. Gagarin was smart, well prepared, and had excellent reactions during emergencies. In 1960, he was chosen to be part of the first group of 20 pilots to train for the Soviet space program.

Gagarin's historic flight lasted 108 minutes and completed one orbit around the Earth. After the mission, he received the title "Hero of the Soviet Union," which was the nation's highest honor. Gagarin never flew in space again, dying tragically in a plane crash in 1968.

"LET'S GO!"

Cosmonaut Yuri Gagarin inside his Soviet Vostok 1 spacecraft.

ALEXEY LEONOV

FIRST SPACEWALK

With the Earth turning below him, cosmonaut Alexey Leonov from the Soviet Union floats outside his spacecraft as he performs history's first spacewalk in 1965.

Cosmonaut Alexey Leonov (1934–), of the Soviet Union, was the first person to leave his spacecraft on an EVA (extravehicular activity). On March 18, 1965, he left the safety of his capsule and floated in the weightlessness of space. Leonov's spacewalk lasted 12 minutes.

The Voskhod 2 mission was a success, but it almost cost Leonov his life. His spacesuit overinflated, and he could not get back inside his spacecraft to rejoin his crewmate, cosmonaut Pavel Belyayev. Thinking quickly, Leonov released air from his suit and was able to squeeze through the hatch before losing consciousness.

Like cosmonaut Yuri Gagarin, Leonov was a military pilot and part of the first group chosen by the Soviet Union to travel in space. After the Voskhod 2 mission, he commanded his country's half of the Apollo-Soyuz Test Project in 1975 with the United States. In addition to his piloting skills, Leonov is a published artist.

Leonov

ALAN SHEPARD

Alan B. Shepard Jr. (1923–1998) was a naval aviator who became the second person—and the first American—to travel into space. He piloted the Mercury *Freedom 7* space capsule. The spacecraft was launched atop a Redstone rocket at Florida's Cape Canaveral on May 5, 1961. Just 10 years later, in 1971, Shepard commanded the Apollo 14 Moon mission. He was the fifth person to walk on the lunar surface, and the first person to hit a golf ball on the Moon. He was also the only one of the original Mercury 7 astronauts to land on the Moon.

Alan Shepard was born on November 18, 1923, in Derry, New Hampshire. While growing up in Derry, he became very interested in flying. He served in the United States Navy during World War II. After the war, Shepard became a Navy test pilot. He flew newly designed aircraft to make sure they were safe for other pilots.

FREEDOM 7

Alan Shepard lifts off in his Mercury space capsule, which he named *Freedom 7*, on May 5, 1961, from Cape Canaveral in Florida.

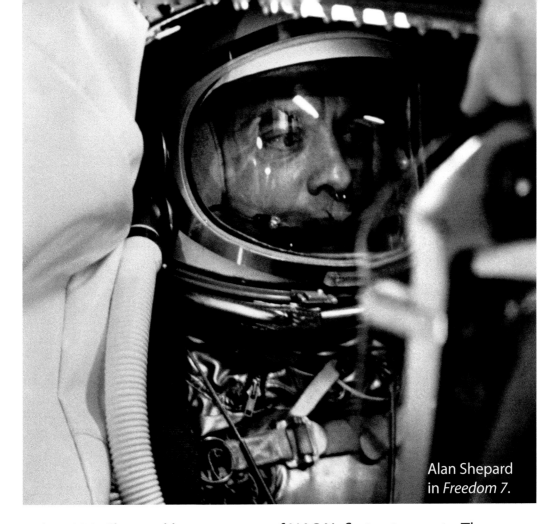

Alan Shepard
in *Freedom 7*.

In 1959, Shepard became one of NASA's first astronauts. They were a group called the Mercury 7. During Shepard's historic Mercury mission, he flew 116 miles (187 km) high. It was a suborbital mission, which means he did not orbit the Earth. However, he was the first person to control his spacecraft in flight (Yuri Gagarin's flight a month earlier was controlled remotely). Shepard's flight lasted about 15 minutes.

After his Apollo 14 mission in 1971, Shepard became the chief of NASA's Astronaut Office. He served briefly at the United Nations and was promoted to rear admiral of the U.S. Navy. In 1974, Shepard retired from NASA and the Navy, but he continued to support space exploration until his death in 1998.

BUZZ ALDRIN

Edwin "Buzz" Aldrin (1930–) is a former NASA astronaut, United States Air Force jet pilot, and engineer. He was the pilot of the Apollo 11 lunar module *Eagle*. On July 20, 1969, he became the second person to walk on the Moon, just a few minutes after mission commander Neil Armstrong. Before the Apollo 11 mission, Aldrin first went into space in 1966, piloting the Gemini 12 spacecraft. He performed three spacewalks totaling 5 hours and 30 minutes, which was a record at the time.

Born Edwin E. Aldrin on January 20, 1930, in Montclair, New Jersey, he was known by his nickname, "Buzz." His father was an aviation pioneer who took Buzz on his first plane ride at age two.

Buzz Aldrin inside the Apollo 11 lunar module.

Growing up in New Jersey, Buzz had a passion for football and hated schoolwork. With his father's help, he eventually became more serious with his studies. He attended the United States Military Academy at West Point, New York. After graduation, he joined the United States Air Force in 1951. During the Korean War, he flew 66 combat missions in F-86 jet fighters. After the war, Aldrin earned a Ph.D. in astronautics from the Massachusetts Institute of Technology.

In 1963, Aldrin became part of the third group of astronauts selected by NASA to train for missions in space. With his engineering and astronautics knowledge, he helped develop tools and skills needed to spacewalk, dock spacecraft, and land safely on the Moon.

After his NASA career, Aldrin became the commander of the United States Air Force Test Pilot School at California's Edwards Air Force Base. He retired in 1972, becoming an author and promoter of space exploration.

MOON EXPLORER

Astronaut Buzz Aldrin standing on the lunar surface, photographed by Neil Armstrong on July 20, 1969 (Armstrong can be seen in Aldrin's faceplate).

JOHN GLENN

Friendship 7 liftoff

In 1962, John Glenn (1921–2016) became the first American astronaut to orbit the Earth. He flew his *Friendship 7* spacecraft three times around the planet. Glenn was a member of the Mercury 7, the first astronauts chosen by NASA. After his astronaut career, he served as a United States senator, representing the state of Ohio from 1974 to 1999. In 1998, while still a senator, he was a crew member on the space shuttle *Discovery*. At age 77, he was the oldest person to ever fly in space.

John Herschel Glenn Jr. was born in Cambridge, Ohio, on July 18, 1921. He flew in an airplane at age eight with his father. That sparked a lifelong love of flying. In 1942, as World War II raged, Glenn put his college education on hold to enlist for military duty. He became a pilot for the United States Marine Corps, flying dozens of combat missions during World War II, the Chinese Civil War, and the Korean War. He earned the Distinguished Flying Cross medal for heroism six times.

In 1954, Glenn became a test pilot, making sure new plane designs were safe to fly. His experience flying military combat jets served him well. After setting aviation speed and distance records, he drew the

READY FOR LIFTOFF

Astronaut John Glenn is helped into his Mercury spacecraft, which he named *Friendship 7*. Glenn orbited the Earth three times in the capsule.

attention of NASA. After intense testing and training, the agency chose him to become an astronaut in 1959.

After his historic Mercury mission, Glenn became a national hero. He was elected to the United States Senate in 1974, representing his home state of Ohio. He was a strong supporter of NASA, nuclear weapons control, and public service. He continued his support of space exploration after retiring from politics in 1999. In 2012, he received the Presidential Medal of Freedom from President Barack Obama. John Glenn died in 2016 at the age of 95.

JOHN YOUNG

John Young (1930–2018) was the longest-serving astronaut in NASA's history. His experience and steady personality earned him legendary respect among other astronauts. He went into space six times during his 42-year career. His missions spanned three major space programs: Gemini, Apollo, and the space shuttle. He walked on the Moon, and commanded the very first space shuttle into orbit. As the chief of NASA's Astronaut Office for 13 years, Young was a tireless supporter of spaceflight training and safety.

LEGEND

John Young was one of the most respected members of NASA's group of astronauts. An experienced test pilot, he flew many kinds of aircraft and spacecraft. He stayed calm under pressure. He also insisted that astronaut safety remain a top NASA priority.

Astronaut John Young, commander of the Apollo 16 Moon mission, leaps from the lunar surface as he salutes the United States flag. The mission's lunar rover can be seen in front of the lunar module spacecraft.

John Watts Young was born in San Francisco, California, on September 24, 1930. He spent most of his childhood in Orlando, Florida. He earned a degree in aeronautical engineering in 1952 from the Georgia Institute of Technology. He soon joined the Navy and served during the Korean War. After the war he became a Navy test pilot. He broke speed and altitude records testing F-4 Phantom II military jets.

In 1962, Young was chosen by NASA to become an astronaut. He trained for many months to prepare for the complexity and dangers of spaceflight. The one-man Mercury program was coming to an end, so Young trained for the two-man Gemini missions.

GEMINI 10

Under a sunny Florida sky, the Gemini 10 spacecraft carrying astronauts John Young and Michael Collins is launched at NASA's Kennedy Space Center on July 18, 1966. The astronauts' main goal was to dock with an unmanned Agena spacecraft that had been sent into orbit earlier. Young and Collins would later use the docking skills they learned on Apollo Moon missions.

John Young suits up before the launch of Gemini 3.

In 1965, Young flew in Gemini 3—the first manned Gemini mission—along with astronaut Gus Grissom. He used his test pilot skills to evaluate the new spacecraft. The mischievous Young also smuggled aboard a corned beef sandwich, which he shared with Grissom. The following year, Young commanded Gemini 10, accompanied by astronaut Michael Collins. They practiced docking with other spacecraft. It was a skill astronauts would later need during the Apollo Moon missions.

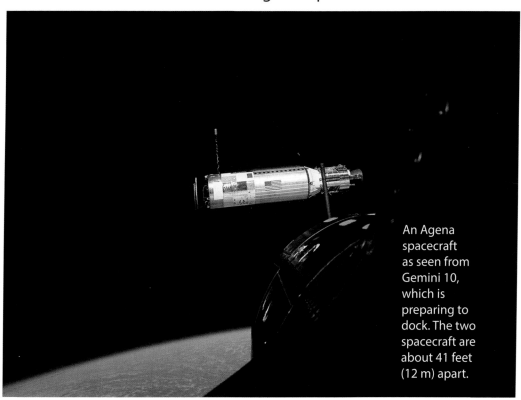
An Agena spacecraft as seen from Gemini 10, which is preparing to dock. The two spacecraft are about 41 feet (12 m) apart.

In May 1969, Young piloted the command module of Apollo 10. He became the first person to fly solo around the Moon. Crewmates Thomas Stafford and Eugene Cernan departed in the lunar module to practice flying a few miles above the Moon. Young stayed behind and controlled the command module alone. When Stafford and Cernan returned, Young used the docking skills he learned in the Gemini program to join the command module with the lunar module. It was the first time two spacecraft docked together while orbiting the Moon. The practice mission was a big success. It paved the way for the historic Apollo 11 Moon-landing mission in July 1969.

In 1972, Young returned to the Moon. He commanded the Apollo 16 mission, which also included crewmates Charles Duke and Ken Mattingly. This time, Young descended to the lunar surface, together with Duke. The pair spent more than 20 hours walking and driving on the Moon. They collected rock samples and performed many science experiments.

Apollo 16's Lunar Roving Vehicle (LRV) gets a speed workout by astronaut John Young.

The first orbital space shuttle flight, STS-1, lifted off from Florida's Kennedy Space Center on April 12, 1981. John Young commanded the orbiter *Columbia* on its 54-hour maiden voyage. He was accompanied by pilot Robert Crippen.

Young served as the chief of NASA's Astronaut Office from 1974 to 1987. He oversaw crew assignments. He also helped test and evaluate NASA's new space shuttle program. In 1981, he commanded the first orbital flight of the *Columbia* spacecraft. In 1983, he again commanded *Columbia* on a 10-day, science-heavy mission with a crew of five other astronauts.

After the space shuttle *Challenger* disaster in 1986, Young worked tirelessly to improve astronaut safety on space shuttles and the International Space Station.

By his retirement in 2004, Young had worked for 42 years for NASA. He flew more than 835 hours in space, but his contributions to the American space program are too great to be measured. John Young died in 2018 at the age of 87.

SCOTT CARPENTER

Scott Carpenter (1925–2013) was the second American to orbit the Earth. His Mercury space capsule, which he named *Aurora 7*, was hurled into space atop an Atlas rocket on May 24, 1962. It was the fourth flight of the Mercury program. Carpenter orbited the Earth three times in a flight lasting nearly five hours.

Carpenter was born in Boulder, Colorado. He was a U.S. Navy jet pilot and flew missions during the Korean War. He later became a test pilot. He was

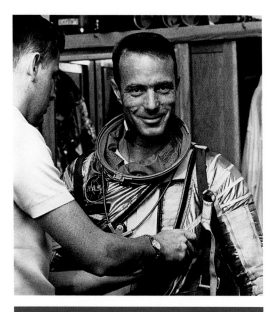

SUITING UP

Astronaut Scott Carpenter is helped into his spacesuit in preparation for his May 24, 1962, Mercury mission. Carpenter was the second American to orbit the Earth.

Aurora 7 lifts off

chosen by NASA in 1959 to become one of the original Mercury 7 astronauts. During his flight in *Aurora 7*, he became the first person to eat food in space. He also performed several science experiments while in orbit.

In 1963, Carpenter joined the Navy's SEALAB project. He spent 30 days in 1965 living in a habitat on the ocean floor. He later used his skills to help astronauts train underwater for spacewalking missions.

GORDON COOPER

Gordon Cooper

Leroy Gordon "Gordo" Cooper Jr. (1927–2004) was one of NASA's original Mercury 7 astronauts. In 1963, he commanded a Mercury spacecraft that he named *Faith 7*. Launched into space on May 15, 1963, it was the last and longest Mercury mission. Cooper flew in space for 34 hours while orbiting the Earth 22 times. He also became the first American astronaut to sleep in space.

Cooper was born and grew up in Shawnee, Oklahoma. He became a U.S. Air Force fighter pilot, and then a test pilot. He was selected to become a Mercury astronaut in 1959, the youngest of the group. During his historic flight, he logged more time than all the previous Mercury missions combined.

In 1965, Cooper traveled to space again, this time with astronaut Charles "Pete" Conrad in Gemini 5. Cooper was the commander of the eight-day mission. They circled the Earth 120 times, proving that humans could survive a long trip to the Moon. Cooper became the first person to make two separate orbital flights around the Earth.

STRAPPED IN

Astronauts Gordon Cooper (left) and Pete Conrad (right) are helped into their Gemini 5 spacecraft just before launch on August 21, 1965.

VALENTINA TERESHKOVA

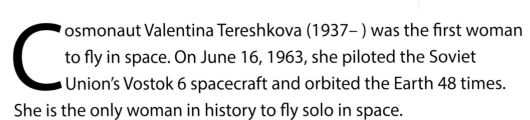

Cosmonaut Valentina Tereshkova (1937–) was the first woman to fly in space. On June 16, 1963, she piloted the Soviet Union's Vostok 6 spacecraft and orbited the Earth 48 times. She is the only woman in history to fly solo in space.

Tereshkova was born in a village in central Russia. She became an expert skydiver, which led to her selection as a cosmonaut. She was chosen from a group of more than 400 applicants to join the Soviet's female cosmonaut corps. She went through intensive training, which included learning to fly jets. She was just 26 years old when she was launched into space.

After her historic three-day spaceflight, Tereshkova became active in politics. She also earned a doctorate degree in engineering.

FIRST WOMAN

Cosmonaut Velentina Tereshkova is suited up before her historic launch into space on June 16, 1963.

GHERMAN TITOV

G herman Titov (1935–2000) was the second Soviet cosmonaut sent into space. On August 6, 1961, he flew solo aboard the Vostok 2 spacecraft. He was 25 years old, which makes him the youngest person ever to fly in space. He was the first person to orbit the Earth multiple times, circling the globe 17 times. During his 25-hour flight, he became the first person to sleep in space. He also was the first to take over manual control of his spacecraft. Even though Titov was a former Soviet air force pilot, he suffered from space sickness, a common kind of motion sickness. That resulted in him in holding another record: the first person to vomit in space.

Gherman Titov

GUS GRISSOM

Gus Grissom (1926–1967) was the second American astronaut to fly in space. He flew in a Mercury spacecraft he named *Liberty Bell 7*. Like Alan Shepard before him, Grissom's 15-minute flight was suborbital, which means it did not circle the Earth. Boosted into space by a powerful Redstone rocket, Grissom's spacecraft reached a height of nearly 103 miles (166 km).

Virgil Ivan "Gus" Grissom was born and grew up in Mitchell, Indiana. He joined the U.S. Air Force and flew 100 combat missions during the Korean War. He then became a test pilot and engineer.

In 1959, Grissom was chosen by NASA to join its first group of astronauts. They were called the Mercury 7. Grissom went through rigorous training to prepare for his *Liberty Bell 7* flight.

Gus Grissom

Grissom was the commander of Gemini 3, along with astronaut John Young. The three-orbit flight, on March 23, 1965, made Grissom the first NASA astronaut to fly in space twice.

Gus Grissom was tragically killed in a launchpad fire on February 21, 1967, during a test of the Apollo 1 Moon mission spacecraft. Also killed were fellow astronauts Edward White and Roger Chaffee.

DEKE SLAYTON

Deke Slayton

Donald "Deke" Slayton (1924–1993) was one of NASA's original Mercury 7 astronauts. Unfortunately, he was grounded because doctors detected an irregular heartbeat. Instead of flying on a Mercury mission, Slayton became the head of NASA's Flight Crew Operations. He was responsible for crew training, and for choosing which astronauts to send on Gemini and Apollo missions.

Slayton was born and grew up near Sparta, Wisconsin. He flew

combat missions during World War II before becoming a test pilot for the U.S. Air Force.

In 1972, Slayton was cleared by doctors to fly once again. Three years later he finally went into space as part of the Apollo-Soyuz Test Project, which included docking with a Soviet spacecraft. At the time, Slayton was the oldest person to fly in space, at age 51.

FINALLY INTO SPACE

A powerful Saturn IB rocket lifts Deke Slayton, along with fellow astronauts Tom Stafford and Vance Brand, into space for their Apollo-Soyuz Test Project mission on July 15, 1975.

WALLY SCHIRRA

Walter "Wally" Schirra (1923–2007) was chosen in 1959 to become part of the elite Mercury 7, the first group of NASA astronauts. He was the only astronaut to fly Mercury, Gemini, and Apollo space missions.

Schirra was born in Hackensack, New Jersey. He studied engineering in school. He learned to fly jets while serving in the military. During the Korean War he flew 90 combat missions. He later became a U.S. Navy test pilot.

As a Mercury astronaut, Schirra became the fifth American to fly in space. On October 3, 1962, his *Sigma 7* spacecraft rocketed into orbit. He flew six times around the Earth before safely splashing down in the Pacific Ocean.

In 1965, Schirra flew on Gemini 6A along with astronaut Tom Stafford. They successfully docked with another Gemini spacecraft. Three years later, Schirra commanded the first manned Apollo flight, Apollo 7, along with Donn Eisele and R. Walter Cunningham. The 11-day mission proved Apollo was ready to travel to the Moon.

TRIPLE THREAT

Astronaut Wally Schirra poses in front of a model of his Mercury spacecraft. He also flew Gemini and Apollo missions.

PETE CONRAD

Pete Conrad on the Moon

Charles "Pete" Conrad Jr. (1930–1999) flew into space four times. Most people remember him today as the commander of Apollo 12. On November 19, 1969, Conrad and Alan Bean became the third and fourth astronauts to land on the surface of the Moon.

Conrad was born in Philadelphia, Pennsylvania. He was very smart, but school was hard for him because he had dyslexia, a reading disability. He found new ways of learning, and eventually earned a degree in aeronautical engineering.

Conrad started flying airplanes when he was a teenager. He joined the U.S. Navy in 1953 and became a fighter pilot. Later, he became a test pilot, which drew the interest of NASA. He was chosen to be an astronaut in 1962.

In addition to his Apollo 12 flight, Conrad flew two Gemini missions and commanded the Skylab 2 space station mission.

SKYLAB 2

Pete Conrad suits up before taking command of the Skylab 2 mission in 1973. Conrad's first name was Charles, after his father, but his mother nicknamed him Peter. Everyone he knew called him Pete.

MICHAEL COLLINS

APOLLO 11 PILOT

While Armstrong and Aldrin walked on the Moon, Collins commanded *Columbia* alone for more than 21 hours. He said he never felt lonely, always a crucial part of the mission.

Michael Collins (1930–) was the command module pilot of NASA's Apollo 11 mission. On July 20, 1969, as fellow astronauts Neil Armstrong and Buzz Aldrin descended to the Moon, Collins stayed behind and flew the command module *Columbia*.

Collins was born in Rome, Italy. His father was a U.S. Army officer stationed overseas. The family lived in many places, but eventually moved to Washington, DC. After graduating from the United States Military Academy at West Point, Collins joined the U.S. Air Force. He trained to became a fighter pilot. Later, he became a highly skilled test pilot.

Collins joined NASA in 1963. On July 18, 1966, he was launched into orbit aboard the Gemini 10 spacecraft. Collins was the pilot. He flew with astronaut John Young, who commanded the mission. They docked with an unmanned Agena spacecraft. These rendezvous skills would later be needed for Apollo Moon missions. During the three-day mission, Collins performed two extravehicular activities (EVA), which made him NASA's third spacewalking astronaut.

FRANK BORMAN

Apollo 8 lifts off

Frank Borman (1928–) commanded Apollo 8, the first manned mission to travel around the Moon. Together with Jim Lovell and Bill Anders, the astronauts blasted off in their Apollo spacecraft on December 21, 1968. It was a dangerous journey that set the stage for later Moon landings. After six days, including 10 orbits around the Moon, the crew returned safely to Earth.

Borman was born in Gary, Indiana, but his family later moved to Tucson, Arizona, where he learned to fly at age 15. After becoming a test pilot for the U.S. Air Force, Borman joined NASA in 1962.

In 1965, Borman commanded Gemini 7, flying along with astronaut Jim Lovell. They set an endurance record of 14 days.

On Christmas Eve, December 24, 1968, as Apollo 8 orbited the Moon, Borman sent this message back home: "And from the crew of Apollo 8, we close with good night, good luck, a Merry Christmas and God bless all of you—all of you on the good Earth."

GEMINI INSPECTION

Astronaut Frank Borman examines his Gemini 7 spacecraft before lifting off on December 4, 1965.

ED WHITE

Edward "Ed" White (1930–1967) was the first American astronaut to leave his spacecraft and "walk" in space. His extravehicular activity (EVA) on the Gemini 4 mission in 1965 was so much fun he didn't want it to end.

White was born and grew up in San Antonio, Texas. He was a bright student and talented athlete. He became a test pilot for the U.S. Air Force in 1959. He joined NASA in 1962.

After the success of Gemini 4, White was chosen to be part of the crew of Apollo 1. Tragically, he and fellow astronauts Gus Grissom and Roger Chaffee died in a launchpad fire on January 27, 1967.

Ed White spacewalking on the Gemini 4 mission.

JIM LOVELL

James "Jim" Lovell (1928–) traveled to space four times during his NASA career, including trips to the Moon twice. He is best remembered as the commander of the ill-fated Apollo 13, which suffered an explosion on board during the trip to the Moon. Thanks to the ingenuity and calm determination of Lovell and crewmates John Swigert and Fred Haise, plus NASA personnel back on Earth, they returned safely on April 17, 1970, after a nail-biting six-day voyage.

Lovell was born in Cleveland, Ohio, but spent much of his childhood in Milwaukee, Wisconsin. He graduated from the United States Naval Academy in 1948, and then trained to become a U.S. Navy jet pilot. A few years later, he became a test pilot, graduating at the top of his class. He tested new aircraft to make sure the designs were safe for other pilots to fly. In 1962, he applied and was accepted by NASA to become an astronaut.

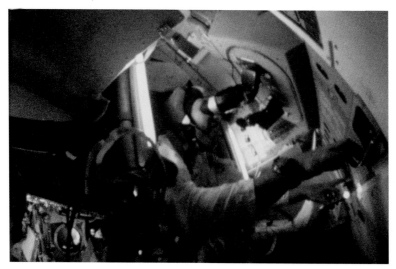

APOLLO 8

Jim Lovell, command module pilot of Apollo 8, at work on the spacecraft's guidance and navigation station during lunar orbit.

Jim Lovell poses in front of the Saturn V rocket and Apollo 8 spacecraft that would take him to the Moon in December 1968.

Lovell's first spaceflight was as the pilot of Gemini 7, along with astronaut Frank Borman. Launched on December 4, 1965, they orbited Earth 206 times over a period of 14 days. The following year Lovell commanded Gemini 12, flying with Buzz Aldrin.

In December 1968, Lovell flew with Frank Borman and William Anders on Apollo 8. Lovell was the command module pilot. It was a risky first voyage to the Moon and back. No human had ever seen the far side of the Moon before. Apollo 8 proved that such a trip was possible.

DAVID SCOTT

David Scott (1932–) flew in space three times. He was the commander of Apollo 15. The mission also included astronauts Alfred Worden and James Irwin. Scott became the seventh person to walk on the Moon. He and Irwin were also the first astronauts to drive on the Moon's surface in a lunar rover.

Scott was born in San Antonio, Texas. He excelled in school and was a star athlete. After a career in the U.S. Air Force flying jet fighters, he joined NASA in 1963. His first spaceflight was with Neil Armstrong aboard Gemini 8 in 1966. He was also the command module pilot for Apollo 9. The 10-day mission included a docking and test flight of the lunar module while in Earth orbit.

APOLLO 9

David Scott stands in the open hatch of the Apollo 9 command module. Scott collected test samples from the spacecraft's exterior. He also took pictures as astronauts James McDivitt and Rusty Schweickart worked on the lunar module.

GENE CERNAN

As the commander of Apollo 17 in December 1972, astronaut Eugene "Gene" Cernan (1934–2017) was the last person to walk on the Moon. He was also one of the few astronauts to travel to the Moon twice. On the Apollo 10 mission in May 1969, Cernan was the lunar module pilot. This rehearsal mission tested all the Apollo systems and hardware, but didn't actually land.

Gene Cernan salutes the American flag during the 1972 Apollo 17 Moon mission.

Cernan was born in Chicago, Illinois. After earning a college degree in electrical engineering, he joined the U.S. Navy and learned to fly jet fighters. He was chosen by NASA to become an astronaut in 1963. His first space mission was as the pilot of Gemini 9A. He also performed a two-hour spacewalk.

Cernan finally made it to the lunar surface during the Apollo 17 mission. As command module pilot Ronald Evans orbited high above, Cernan and fellow astronaut Harrison Schmitt collected rock samples and conducted science experiments. They spent more than three days on the Moon, a record that stands to this day.

PEGGY WHITSON

Peggy Whitson (1960–) was the first female commander of the International Space Station (ISS). She is NASA's most experienced astronaut, with more than 665 days in space. She has spacewalked 10 times, for a total of more than 60 hours. That gives her the record for most extravehicular activities (EVAs) by a woman. She was 57 years old during her last mission on the ISS in 2017, which made her the oldest woman astronaut in space.

Whitson was born in Mount Ayr, Iowa, and grew up on a farm near Beaconsfield. She earned a doctorate degree in biochemistry. She began working for NASA in 1989 as a biochemist. A dedicated scientist and explorer, she started astronaut training in 1996.

Starting with her first trip to the ISS in 2002 as a science officer, Whitson made a total of three long-duration missions to the space station. She was also the chief of NASA's Astronaut Office from 2009 to 2012. Whitson retired from NASA in June 2018.

Peggy Whitson in the Cupola of the International Space Station.

GUY BLUFORD

Guion "Guy" Bluford (1942–) is the first African American to fly in space. He was a mission specialist on four space shuttle missions. His first was in August 1983 aboard the space shuttle *Challenger*. He and the other four astronauts aboard released a communications satellite and tested the remote Canadarm robotic arm system. Bluford also flew on space shuttle missions in 1985, 1991, and 1992. In total, he logged more than 688 hours in orbit around the Earth.

Bluford was born in Philadelphia, Pennsylvania. He was very interested in science in school. He eventually earned a doctorate degree in aerospace engineering.

Bluford became a U.S. Air Force pilot in 1966. He flew 144 combat missions during the Vietnam War. He was also a flight instructor. He logged more than 5,200 hours of jet flying time.

After retiring from NASA in 1993, Bluford worked for several aerospace companies.

SHUTTLE DISCOVERY

The space shuttle *Discovery*, with Guy Bluford and four other astronauts aboard, lifts off from Florida's Kennedy Space Center on December 2, 1992, for a seven-day secret military mission.

CHRIS HADFIELD

Canadian astronaut Chris Hadfield (1959–) flew on two space shuttle missions and later served as commander of the International Space Station (ISS) from March to May 2013. He is the first Canadian to walk in space.

Hadfield was born in Sarnia, Ontario, and grew up on a farm in the southern part of the province. He learned to fly glider aircraft at age 15. After joining the Canadian Armed Forces, he earned a mechanical engineering degree and learned to fly combat fighter jets. He later became a test pilot before joining the Canadian Space Agency, where he trained to become an astronaut.

One of Hadfield's goals is to educate the public about the importance of space exploration. He famously released a music video in 2013 of himself playing guitar in the ISS and singing David Bowie's "Space Oddity." The video has been seen by tens of millions of people on Youtube and other social media outlets.

TRAINING

Canadian astronaut Chris Hadfield posing next to a T-38 jet. The T-38 is a two-seat, supersonic jet that is used as a training aircraft in several countries.

Chris Hadfield playing the guitar inside the International Space Station's Cupola viewing dome.

LEROY CHIAO

Leroy Chiao (1960–) was selected in 1990 by NASA to become an astronaut. He eventually had a 15-year career with the space agency. He has flown into space four times. He was a mission specialist on three space shuttle flights. He also commanded the International Space Station (ISS) from October 2004 to April 2005. He was the first Asian-American to command the ISS. In total, he logged more than 229 days in space.

Chiao was born in Milwaukee, Wisconsin, but grew up in Danville, California. Both of his parents are immigrants from the Republic of China (Taiwan). He is a native English speaker, but also speaks fluent Mandarin Chinese and Russian. These skills have helped him train and consult with scientists from other countries, and to communicate with cosmonauts on the ISS. Chiao has several advanced science degrees, and is a trained pilot. After his career with NASA, Chiao became an author and engineering consultant.

TRAINING

Astronaut Leroy Chiao spent more than 229 days in space on shuttle missions and as commander of the International Space Station.

SALLY RIDE

stronaut Sally Ride (1951-2012) was born and raised in Los Angeles, California. She joined NASA in 1978, beating out thousands of applicants for the chance to become an astronaut. Five years later, on June 18, 1983, she rode the space shuttle *Challenger* into orbit around the Earth, becoming the first American woman to travel into space. She was a mission specialist who helped deploy communications satellites and conduct scientific experiments. She flew on *Challenger* again in 1984. She logged a total of more than 14 days in space during her career.

Challenger liftoff, June 18, 1983.

Despite her history-making flight as the first female astronaut, Ride was proud to simply to call herself an astronaut and let her accomplishments speak for themselves. After her NASA career, Ride worked as an author and teacher.

Sally Ride working inside the space shuttle *Challenger*.

SCOTT KELLY

Scott Kelly (1964–) flew into space four times during his 20-year astronaut career. He is best known for his nearly year-long stay aboard the International Space Station (ISS). He and Russian cosmonaut Mikhail Korniyenko were chosen to test the affects of long periods of weightlessness on the human body. In addition to his spaceflight experience, Kelly was chosen because he had a twin brother, Mark (who was also an astronaut). Mark remained on Earth. Each had their eyesight, blood, urine, and other body systems checked for differences. The tests were done to find out if humans could live in space for long periods of time. This information may help with future missions to faraway planets such as Mars.

Kelly was born in Orange, New Jersey. He learned to fly jets in the U.S. Navy and became a test pilot. During his NASA career, he flew the space shuttle twice, and also commanded the ISS. He spent a total of 520 days in space, including 18 hours of spacewalking.

ISS VIEW

Astronaut Scott Kelly takes a selfie inside the Cupola viewing dome of the International Space Station. The Earth can be see far below through one of the Cupola's windows.

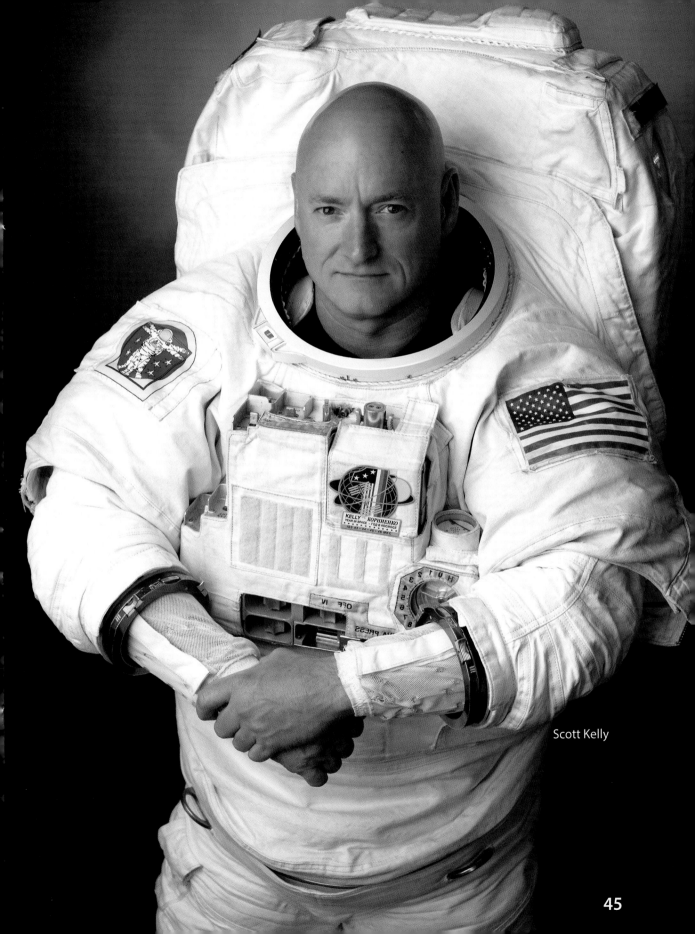

Scott Kelly

GLOSSARY

Astronaut

Someone who travels in a spacecraft. The word has Greek roots that stand for "star sailor" or "star traveller."

Canadarm

The Canadarm and Canadarm2 robotic arm systems were developed and made in Canada. Canadarm was used on the space shuttle. Canadarm2 is currently used on the International Space Station (ISS) to help assemble and repair ISS modules. It can also capture and dock unmanned supply spacecraft.

Cosmonaut

An astronaut from Russia or the former Soviet Union.

Cupola

A dome-shaped module on the ISS. It is attached to the larger Tranquility module. It was built in Italy and attached to the ISS in 2010. Its large windows give astronauts a panoramic view of the Earth. The circular central window is 31.5 inches (80 cm) in diameter, the largest window ever used in space.

National Aeronautics and Space Administration (NASA)

A United States government space agency started in 1958. NASA's goals include space exploration and increasing people's understanding of Earth, our solar system, and the universe.

ORBIT

The circular path a moon or spacecraft makes when traveling around a planet or other large celestial body. The International Space Station takes about 90 minutes to make one complete orbit around the Earth.

SOVIET UNION

A former country that included a union of Russia and several other communist republics. It was formed in 1922 and existed until 1991.

SPACE SHUTTLE

American's first reusable space vehicle. NASA built five orbiters: *Columbia, Challenger, Atlantis, Discovery*, and *Endeavour*. Two shuttles and their crews were destroyed by accidents: *Challenger* in 1986, and *Columbia* in 2003.

TEST PILOT

A person who flies new or experimental aircraft to test the machine's flight worthiness and to make sure it is safe for other pilots to fly.

ONLINE RESOURCES

Booklinks
NONFICTION NETWORK
FREE! ONLINE NONFICTION RESOURCES

To learn more about astronauts and cosmonauts, visit **abdobooklinks.com** or scan this QR code. These links are routinely monitored and updated to provide the most current information available.

INDEX